Sun Showers

Tamica Northcutt

BookLeaf Publishing

Presentation by *BookLeaf Publishing*

Web: www.bookleafpub.com

E-mail: info@bookleafpub.com

ISBN: 9789357696708

First edition 2023

DEDICATION

For you.

Because when one chapter ends

inevitably another begins.

Three AM

Nothing good ever happens at this time
It's too quiet too dark
And I'm left alone to my own devices
There are the pictures that I was never in
The questions and the endless alternate endings to the
conversation that has already been had
Decisions have been made
Nothing good ever happens at this time
Yet sometimes I welcome it instead of sleep
Just because you're there

To My Person

You reminded me of something. There are going to
be times when I feel absolutely lost. When I look
around me and have no idea what I want or where I
am going. Moments where I feel like I have done
nothing, will be nothing, and deserve nothing.
And I will remember you.
Not because you told me I could be anything or that I
would preserver. But because you saw me when I was
there, head barely above water, always contemplating
letting go and floating out to sea. You saw me and
never denied or tried to save me. Because you knew
there would come a day when you wouldn't be there
to toss the rope. You wouldn't be there to help me
strap on my life jacket.
You did not save me.
You let me go until I had a reason to save myself.
And as much as I may have wanted it to be, you
knew that reason could not be you.

Meet and Greet

I will be my own worst enemy
Determined to make you see all the flaws all the time
And be happy once you do
But then you're gone
And I realize that I wanted you
But was never comfortable with you wanting me.

HER

Has anyone ever called you a muse? Pandora herself?
Tease
A magical box filled with such sins
Harlot
You gave me a taste of what has inspired ballads of
undying love and eternal hate all in the same breath
That which has broken homes and turned the most
stoic atheist into a believer on scabbed knees
Worshiped
To be kicked out of that temple
Left neglected, a babe no longer able to suck at the tit
for nourishment.
What sacrifice is appropriate? What offering will you
have?
Slut
Leave your mark for others
Tighten the ropes if you must
A proper punishment indeed.

S.A.M.

Just one more time
Bend me
Bite me
Put your hands right where I like them
Tight
Hold me just enough to let me sink
My body shivers
Your words, commands, questions, demands
I wish I could see your face
Delight?
Disgust?
Disappointment?
Entertained?
Excited?
Pleasure.

Mirror

There will always be those unsaid words. That is the nature of this beast. Would things have been different? Of course. Maybe.

But that means I would have had to be different. You would have had to be different. And we weren't there. And so here we are waiting to see who is going to fold first. The olive branch wrapped in a white flag.

Eleven/Twenty Seventeen

I still miss you because no one has replaced you. Yet. I
knew this wouldn't be easy. Nothing has been as easy as us.
The talks aren't there. The care isn't there.
It is rather easy to be open. Very hard to be vulnerable. I
told you I loved you and meant it. You offered me no
promises. You never asked me to wait. I told you I loved
you anyway. Looking back, that took courage that maybe I
don't have today.

Patience. Compromise. I don't like it here without you.

Can you come back?

Unmedicated

This isn't a place that you know
Still
Dark, cold, numb, false
Yet here it is warm and soft
Your thoughts are just mere whispers, tiny echoes of
doubt
Different. Unpleasant at times but necessary.
What has happened to the you that you knew?
She's gone
And who is this new person?

Sun Shower

We were that.
Three things that should not have existed at the same
time in the same place. A phenomenon. Sun. Rain.
Rainbow.

Why did we think we were ever going to survive?
Why did we think we were special?

Dear Dolores

fuck you

Selfish

What if this was our time
No next lifetime since the universe does not play favorites
And I lost you
I was never on your timeline, yet you defined mine
And no one won
Because death does not play fair or keep count
It ignores prayers and cries and broken hearts
Rage became acceptance
And now when I see a picture of the two of you, I smile
Because we each had our time
Each played our part in your life's play
She your rock, your nurse, your light
Me your chaos, your release, your dark
And I can and do smile
Because you wouldn't have it any other way

Honor

Say those words you know I need to hear
Bruise all the right places
Your voice stirs something deep within my core
Make me sit at attention
Always an honor

Paris

It's okay. Sometimes it will hurt. And sometimes it won't. Sometimes I may forget to even think about it. I had plans. Places to go. Experiences I wanted to share. I can still do those things. I can still go to those places.

It just won't be with you.

Exit

I loved your love
It was something so different and new
It was never something for me though
Always on the outside looking in
And you let me watch
Front row ticket yet somehow always last to the show and
sitting in the back
Did my name even make the credits?
Standing ovation for the cast and crew.
So good, I watched it again even after the first run left me
hollow and aching
Flowers and accolades to all involved
Bow and curtsy if you will
I will go out the way I came in
You'll never know I was there

Lesson One

I noticed how my breathing changed
How my pulse quickened
How my defenses went down
There were no questions
I knew less than a novice
I was a blank slate, impressionable, eager, unsuspecting
hardly innocent, a very willing pupil
Teach me
Train me
Bind me

Assignment

You wanted my words
and they were yours to have
about you about us
I wrote and waited
Waited and wrote
In the end I wanted my words back
they were mine to begin
You were the spark, the fuel, the Keeper
A bomb I did not expect
So you can have them
They were earned
Lovely parting gifts. A memento perhaps?
More than what you left for me.

Here

But oh, if these walls could speak
The delicious debauchery within its space
Such an unassuming place
Birthday parties, celebrations, family movie nights
bedtime stories and sweet goodnight kisses
But oh, these walls
slick with sweat
the air moist from hot labored breaths
So many secrets, whispered pleas, moans
Other unnatural sounds
This is where it all began.
Home Sweet Home

Tell Me

I came when called
Kneeled when told
My neck was yours to hold
You wanted loyalty with no expiration date
I just wanted you to be my peace in the storms
But you became the storm
And when your winds of discontent blew open the doors
I ran
Because I refused to rust
I was never playing checkers or chess
I wanted you to be right and prove me wrong
I never wanted to best you
But I didn't know how to just give you me

Last Call

Funny how blame works. Who said it was a bad thing? Accusatory. A defense. Like the lotus grows in mud, I grow in blame. I see the whole thing. Not just you but me too. Blame gives me breathing room and space because it can be exhausting trying to be right all the time. Rumor has it no one wants to take the blame. They try to push it off, hide from it, shame other with it.

Leave it with me.

You don't have to wrap it up or make it pretty or pair it with a chaser.

Straight. Sloppy. Sweet. Sour. Give it to me.

www.ingramcontent.com/pod-product-compliance
Lightning Source LLC
LaVergne TN
LVHW021353200726
843509LV00014B/2822